Unmasked

Unmasked

Yahya Al-Abed, M.D.

GOLDEN ARROW PUBLISHING

UNMASKED

Copyright © 2017 by Yahya Al-Abed

Cover Art by Spiffing Covers

Published by Golden Arrow Publishing, California

www.GoldenArrowPublishing.com

ISBN: 978-1975862732

FIRST EDITION

To Mum and Rapunzel

Contents

1 THE ACCIDENT 9

2 THE AMBULANCE RIDE.................................... 25

3 THE WAITING ROOM 33

4 THE DIAGNOSIS 43

5 THE ADMISSION... 55

6 THE SURGERY 63

7 THE RECOVERY ROOM..................................... 79

8 DISCHARGED 91

9 HOME AGAIN... 101

10 ADAPTING 115

11 BACK TO WORK 127

1 The Accident

It was my own fault. I should have never agreed to cover extra rounds at the hospital on a work out day but the service floor manager seemed desperate as a couple of the other doctors had called in sick at the last minute. The never-ending influx of patients wouldn't attend to themselves so I stuck around a few extra hours to help out, even though my night shift was over. Unfortunately, that meant there was a good chance I'd be late to my appointment with my coach at the ice rink.

Skating was turning out to be a great outlet of mine and I was turning out to be better than both my mother and I had anticipated. Even with her living back home in the Emirates while I worked in London, she had a way of being heard. She declared early on that hockey was a viciously dangerous, precarious sport only meant for people with anger issues and a lust for competition. I should be finding a safer form of exercise that didn't involve beating up other players with a stick. It made absolutely no difference when I told her I was actually learning how to figure skate. My attempts to ease her concerns were only met with indignation and a long list of facts highlighting the dangers of frolicking on the ice. Although, over the years, she's turned out to be one of my biggest, silent supporters as she saw how much fun I was having. Or, perhaps, it's because I simply chose not to bring the topic up very often.

I valued the sport for so much more than its physical component and its ability to keep my body healthy. Skating had become my form of mediation, a mental release from everything else that was going on during my days both personally and at work. It was the noise of solitude that gripped me and kept me coming back. It's similar to skiing down a mountain alone and hearing only the sound of fresh powder making way under your feet. It's just you focusing on the winter wonderland at your feet.

My last patient of the evening was a gentleman in his early 40's who overestimated the strength of an old, wooden ladder found in his grandfather's garage. He came in with a few splinters on his head and concerns that he'd given himself a concussion when he lost his footing and slammed his head against a shelf. What he was doing on a ladder in the middle of the night was beyond me. But, good news for him, though. The tests came back negative. However, I still wouldn't trade places with that hefty bruise that'll linger on his forehead for a week or two.

Leaving him with instructions for a quick recovery, I make my way to the locker room to change when I get a call from Sandra, my junior doctor. Time to reroute. A 70-year-old male is in resuscitation in the Emergency Room with a perforated colon. After assessing the scans, I confirm surgery is imminent for his survival and give the operating theatre's staff the go ahead to begin preparations.

And to think, I actually thought my night shift would end on a quiet note. My stomach begins growling audibly and my junior looks over at me inquisitively.

"Sounds like a bear out of hibernation," she jests.

"Let's get out of here," I command.

"Where are we going?" she stumbles behind me.

"Food. We need it. I can't have these stomach protests distracting me during surgery. While the patient is being prepped, we have enough time to drive through the only place that's open this early in the morning."

"McDonald's?"

"McDonald's."

Racing over to our gourmet breakfast, we're able to swallow a burger and some coffee – quality at its finest. Depending on the day, taking a break to eat isn't always on the schedule, so these few moments to grab some sustenance actually feel like a bonus. My junior and I revel in our own glory as we proudly accept the number one and number two status McDonald's has bestowed upon us. It may have merely been a number on our receipts indicated the first orders of the day, but we beat out thousands of other people and didn't hesitate to do a little dance when exiting.

Back at the hospital and four hours later, the patient is in recovery after a successful surgery. Once again, I revel in my success. There are few things more satisfying than knowing you helped save a person's life. The older gentleman would be alright although he would require some extensive monitoring in intensive care compared to someone younger in age.

Well into the morning now, I see the sun shining through the hospital windows and the rest of the world populating the already busy London streets. If I went directly to the ice rink rather than stopping by my flat first, I could probably manage to get in a solid warm up before my coach, Mandy, started on my balancing drills. Perhaps today we'd have time to work on the toe loop jump and maybe even push the limits with a single axel.

I could already hear the echoes of Mandy's laughter as I playfully demand permission to perform harder drills. I might as well ask for a double axel because there was no way I was ready. My constant need to push my own limitations kept me in a state of wishful thinking. I was well on my way towards a gold level of skating but it was good that she kept me grounded so I could get there in one piece. I would have to work much harder to enter the professional arena and that wasn't going to happen anytime soon with only two lessons a week. All my time working at the hospital didn't allow me to train any more than that.

Passing the front desk, I wave at the remaining night shift workers still collecting their things. It was easy to spot those colleagues who were asked to work longer hours because of their exhausted, sluggish movements. Attending to patient needs could weigh you down after just a few hours and most of us had been there for a solid twelve assessing the well-being of every person who came through our doors. We solve problems just like any other business except we do it in a building that is forever an iconic symbol for emotional intensity. Working with someone's health means you are dealing with so much more than the human body. You are dealing with the human mind as well. We are constantly subjected to a pendulum of emotions that alter the temperature of our own mental state as if being submerged under hot and cold water every time we change patient rooms.

London is also known for having an eclectic population with different backgrounds, cultures, personal and religious viewpoints. To these people, we are continually delivering good news, bad news, life-altering news and, sometimes, almost incomprehensible news. You've got your high-risk patients and low-risk patients, your in and out patients or the ones who must stay with us for a few days.

You may be lucky and have a patient who listens, eager to learn and who is ready to take your professional recommendations. Or, perhaps, you may get blessed with the kind of patient who swears up and down the hospital hallways that they know more than the doctors because the internet told them so. They've Googled their symptoms and nothing can trump that. Regardless of the patient personality, no matter who walks through that door, each one will receive the best "free at the point of use" treatment the National Health Service (NHS) can give.

Needless to say, there's enough to overwhelm the psyche in the medical field and cause even the most experienced professionals to search for their happy place, which was exactly why I was now rushing out the door. No one had to twist my arm to take a break.

I deserved a mini getaway too after finishing my specialty training in colon and rectal surgery that was complimented my general knowledge. That was over a month ago and I still hadn't found the time to celebrate with friends during my job hunt for a new position. But, until my next extended vacation, I'd have to content myself with a general ice, cold working out.

Although, figure skating is far from mundane. Rather, it was my escape. At work, I was on the clock as a medical professional with a high level of responsibility and obligation to anyone and everyone with a slight bruise to advanced cancer. When I finally had a few days off to regroup, I was busy catching up on all those bedtime Z's I had missed during my shifts which left little time for a social life.

The stress of it all became a distant memory as the double doors of the skating arena opened and a swift chill made its way out past me to greet the coming festivities of the winter months. It may have only been October, but Christmas and New Year's would be here before I knew it. Losing track of time – one of many occupational hazards.

There were a few extra people on the ice today, including my coach, Mandy, who was finishing a lesson with another skater. That wouldn't stop me from warming up though. I quickly lace up my skates, eager to feel the ice beneath the blades. Here we go… Slight lean left, gentle push right. Single turn here and double turn there. Free skate. Balance on left, rotate on right.

"Don't look down. Keep your shoulders level!"

I could already hear Mandy's voice instructing me from the sidelines. My lesson hadn't even started yet but she always found her way into my head. Good coaches have a way of doing that.

"Jump like a man! Land like a lady."

That one was my favourite. I used to chuckle every time I heard it until I finally realised how right she was. There was a combination of power and elegance needed to perform most tricks. What separates the champions from the amateurs is consistently being able to find the perfect balance between the two. Or, so I'm told.

I still remember my first glide across the ice. Or, perhaps, it was more of a wobble – an elephant wearing skates kind of ordeal. My interest was piqued a few years back when I was driving to and from my specialist training at the hospital. During the later months of the year, my daily drive took me past a scenic, outdoor skating rink in the centre of town with towering buildings all around it. The festivities forced your eye to rest upon the colourful decorations and Christmas lighting strewn above. Wanting to join in, I bought tickets and invited a date to go along with me. The fact that I had never skated in my entire life was completely beside the point. I should have been embarrassed for nearly falling over and over again in front of my date but I was too distracted by the other skaters all around me who seemed to float effortlessly across the ice. I wanted to be able to do that, too. And, there's no reason why I shouldn't be. Challenge accepted!

A few months later, my lessons were well under way. I soon went from hardly being able to stand up straight, fumbling in my infancy, to gliding becoming second nature. I grew at ease with my environment, my insecurities no longer hindering my progress. It's not merely the slippery surface to contend with but my own level of confidence. I finally made the decision to not let anything limit my progress anymore.

Hearing Mandy call out to me, I go to end my warm-up with one last jump but a loud, cracking noise within the stadium interrupts my concentration and my balance goes off kilter. My skates stumble across the ice, the blades searching for the ground for stability as my arms aggressively swing around my body, making every attempt to recover. With nothing to grab onto, not even a fellow skater passing by, I lose all control as gravity takes hold and viciously pulls me straight down to an unforgiving surface.

These are the moments I don't love sports as much as I should. Why couldn't I fall on some fluffy pillows or a pile of leaves? Tripping onto dirt is even less painful than this. Instead, I'm flat on my tummy, involuntarily hugging the ice as its chill soaks through my sleeves. What did I do wrong? One second I'm gracefully mastering basic skills and the next, the ice is aggressively reminding me to stay humble.

Opening my eyes, I lift my chest up far enough to watch my breath float across the frozen surface towards a distinctive patch of ice missing from the floor beneath me. It was a small, jagged area I had skated over, no more than an inch or two wide. It was probably chipped by another skater's fall but had not been properly smoothed over. I reach my hand out to feel how deep the ice gash is when I begin to hear something other than my own thoughts.

"Are you ok?" Mandy asks urgently.

My tunnel vision on the broken ice caused me to miss the people now trickling in overhead. I prop myself up further to look at the concerned faces starring down at me. They must have heard the noise, too.

"Yahya?! Are you all right?" Mandy repeats.

Was I all right? Of course, I was all right. Does ice thaw after the winter season? Are doctors overworked? Was sitting on the ice dampening my undergarments? Of course! Falls happen all the time. You sign up for them when you sign up for lessons. In fact, they are such a big part of the game that figure skaters are taught how to fall properly early on to minimize the potential damage in the future.

It was a little dramatic for so many strangers to come check on me and my mouth opens to allay their fears, the way I always would after a rough patch was hit. Although, this time, I was so distracted with shrugging off their attention that I hadn't even noticed my hands cradling my left ankle in unbearable pain.

"No," I shake my head, rather dumbfounded. "I don't think I'm alright at all."

A few onlookers help me to the side and I fall onto a bench, grabbing it for support as I feel another sharp pain shoot through my leg. Managing to move me into a sitting position, Mandy gently removes my skate to assess the damage. She couldn't hide her true feelings as she witnessed my ankle changing colour right in front of her eyes. Secretly wishing to avoid the truth, I look down to see for myself.

Medical Observational Assessment: Swelling and blue discoloration suggests high blood concentration around and/or within the joint. Increased pain and sensitivity to touch denotes

21

possible bone fracture. Likelihood of severe damage to the surrounding ligaments – practically guaranteed. Extent of injuries to adjoining body parts – to be determined. Chance of fainting – unknown.

No! This can't be happening! I have to go to work later tonight! Patients need to be seen. I need to walk. Walking is an essential part of my job. It's an essential part of living! My last jump would have been absolutely perfect if the rest of my body had cared enough to join the rotation. Instead, I jumped and landed on the one, tiny section of the entire ice rink that changed my fate and turned me into a helpless rag doll. What were the odds of that happening?

And, that sound. It was the worst kind of noise you could possibly hear; worse than screeching car tyres or fingernails on a chalkboard. Rather, this was an internal noise. A kind of cracking that runs through your body, muscle to muscle, nerve to nerve, and all the way to your brain forcing your eyes to shut so tight that you desperately pretend you can dream the pain away.

What had just happened?

"Yahya!" My coach snaps me back to reality. "Think fast. It's time to make some decisions."

2 The Ambulance Ride

There was a moment of silence as I agreed with what everyone around me was thinking. The pain I was feeling was more than just a sprain. It was clear that I needed to go directly to the hospital and as quickly as possible. But, how does this work? What am I supposed to do? As far as I could remember, I'd never been in this situation before, not even as a child. I was always more of a tinker with tools child rather than a jump off the roof kind. That might explain why I became a surgeon rather than a stunt double.

No one knew what was going through my mind. So many thoughts were flooding in; accepting that I have a broken ankle, leaving my car unattended, unable to go to work and what hospital to go to. Clearly, I can't drive to the emergency room so I'll need to call someone. But, who would be able to pick me up at this time of the day? It's early in the day when most people are working and I have no family in town. Actually, I had no family in the country at all. My parents and siblings can't do anything for me from 4,000 miles away.

A spectator close by begins calling an ambulance but I quickly stop them. I knew I couldn't force the ambulance to go to the hospital I wanted and they'll automatically take me to the emergency room closest to the skating arena. I knew that particular hospital well and it didn't have as good a reputation compared to a few others. I would opt for a higher level of quality care if I could help it, especially if I had to be operated on.

The emergency dispatch team also won't consider a fractured ankle to be an emergency like they do a heart attack or even a drunk person with potential alcohol poisoning vomiting outside a local pub. Of course I would be considered a low-priority, which means they probably wouldn't show up for several hours. I couldn't wait that long.

I fiddle around in my duffel bag in search of my phone. I would contact the only person I knew who would come right away; a proven saviour to me on more than one occasion; the only person I could rely on who would willingly and without question show up within five minutes – an Uber cab driver.

With my personal ambulance on its way, it was time to find someone who could take my car home. I called the only person I knew who wasn't working, my doctor friend Yasmin. She's such a busy person but still manages to help me out.

A few moments later, a black, Toyota Prius (a classic Uber staple) pulls up outside the skating rink. My coach helps me stagger out to the curb where, upon closer inspection, I see a large, scratched up dent on the side of the vehicle.

"That's reassuring," I muttered to myself as I fell into the passenger's seat. This isn't the most comforting car decal I've ever seen but at least this transportation would be faster than waiting for a real ambulance. I give the destination to the driver and we're off.

On a normal trip, I would be engaged in conversation with my escort, but there was no time for idle chitchat when my mobile phone was ringing tirelessly and bouncing around the car from my pocket, to the seat, to the floor like some overdosed jumping bean.

"I don't know where to park your car!" my friend screams on the other end. Damn London parking!

"Be careful, Yasmin. The shifting can be tricky. Sensitive clutch."

"Don't worry," she laughs. "I've only stalled twice."

The Uber car was jolted by a pothole and the resulting surge of pain prevented me from having a sense of humour. Trying to balance my injured leg on the other wasn't working as well as I had hoped and the pain was intensifying. I direct Yasmin to my usual parking spot and hang up to find my driver tense at the wheel.

"I'm not very good at this stuff," he hesitates. "Hospital stuff. The blood, the needles. I don't like it."

Great. This guy is a wimp. To be fair, he had no idea he was picking up a broken person. Maybe I should have saved some money and taken the ambulance after all. That was definitely one of the benefits of a free healthcare system. But, there is no reason to change drivers now. I didn't need him to *like* taking me to the hospital, I just needed him to do it anyway.

More importantly, I needed my driver to take me to my hospital of choice, the place where I recently finished my surgical specialty training just a month prior. I was familiar with their standard of care and could be assured of their capabilities and professionalism. It was one of the best urgent care centres in the country and I couldn't imagine being treated anywhere else.

Another pothole attacks the Prius and sends more pain racing through my leg. We were no match for the condition of these roads but squeezing the door handle helped me regroup. It wasn't as comforting as a human hand but it would have to do.

"You're a grown man, Yahya. You better not scream. Keep it together," I kept reminding myself. I wondered if the driver heard my pain. I would hold in there if he would, too. We had over five miles to go and, in London traffic, that meant over 45 minutes of driving and probably a thousand more potholes to cover.

Ignoring my driver's confession, I call another friend, an old colleague who still worked at the hospital I was headed to. He assured me that he would alert the staff to my situation and expedite everything upon my arrival. Wonderful! Although, why is it just now occurring to me that all my friends are doctors? It wasn't a bad group to have close by, but I clearly needed to get out more.

Relief flooded my system when I saw the hospital building come into view and I immediately instructed the Uber driver to park in the ambulance bay. I figured there was no quicker way to get attention than by parking somewhere you're not supposed to. Within seconds an angry nurse runs out, arms flailing and demands the driver move his vehicle.

"It's my fault. I'm a doctor here. I've been injured and I need a wheelchair immediately."

My plan was working.

3 The Waiting Room

A nurse wheels me into the waiting room where I make eye contact with several people sitting amongst two, maybe three dozen indistinguishable clones scattered throughout, all waiting to be seen. They all appeared impatiently powerless to break through the first line of hospital defence, the receptionist and visit with the only person they truly wanted to see, the doctor.

If this process truly is first come first serve, I really am in big trouble. Good thing I called ahead and had them prep for my arrival. I look up at the nurse who finished backing my wheelchair against the wall right beside a trash bin that had clearly been fed leftovers from the vending machine across the room. I could pick up a combination scent of half-eaten cheese sandwiches, stale chocolate bars and rejected, burnt coffee. And people thought the smell of formaldehyde was bad. I was sure there was a hint of spiced jerky but my gag reflex wouldn't let me think on it any longer. And, I work in colon surgery. What does that tell you?

I make my attempt to cut the wait line.

"I need to go to the Urgent Care unit."

"I'll send someone over from the booking station to collect your information," the nurse skilfully evades my instruction.

Not pleased with her dismissive tone, I grab my phone realising now was probably as good a time as any to call my family and fill them in on what was happening.

"Hey, Dad. I've had a little accident and I'm at the hospital now."

Before I can get through the whole story, I hear my mother and sister crying in the background, each trying to grab their turn on the telephone.

"Does this make you happy?!" my mother sobs into my ear. "Are you going to stop skating now?!"

"No way! I'm not going to stop doing what I love just because of something like this. Accidents happen all the time."

I wasn't being very sensitive to my mother's frantic state. I also wasn't sure my words were true and that I would even be capable of returning to the sport. The initial, less invasive assessment is one thing, but my medical experience taught me that there was no way to be sure about the full extent of any injury until a thorough assessment had been completed. There was a small chance that I may have injured a part of my body that could end my sporting ambitions indefinitely. This one accident could bring them to an abrupt halt as quickly as my fall to the ice had been.

I shifted uncomfortably in my chair as I relived the afternoon's poor performance and forced myself to comprehend the worst-case scenario. If my ankle was permanently damaged, figure skating would be only one of many activities I wouldn't be able to do anymore.

I attempted to end the conversation with my parents as quickly as possible, as if I had somewhere more important to be. In reality, I was stuck in a waiting area that was in no way meant for someone in my condition with potentially broken body parts. This was just a booking location where they collect your personal information and they weren't even doing that! What was going on in the back room, anyway? They were probably slacking off, playing games and checking their social media accounts. Who knows?

How strange that they would just leave me here to grow indignant and stare at the clock as it stole time from me. Did they not receive the priority message that I was a doctor with a broken ankle? I was growing more irritable by the minute. There had to be someone around here who knew me and could get the ball rolling.

I was never quick to anger like so many other customers who received unsatisfactory service but the appeal was beginning to grow on me. Those people always get what they want. The impatient coffee addict who screams at the barista when the order is not made to their exact specifications or the complainer who gets their meal complimentary because they purposefully and publicly complain about their displeasing dish.

Just as I finished re-evaluating my moral code, a young worker passing by recognises me.

"You've been here before," he states but unsure where to place me in his memory.

"Indeed. I was a doctor here."

"Oh my! I'll go send a nurse for you," and he scurries away.

Just a few moments later, a nurse comes out of the back room and I raise my head in eager anticipation of her calling my name next. No luck. The woman sitting across from me, with an incessant cough, stood up to claim her visit with the doctor.

With a rough diagnosis, I could have spared her the wait and written her a prescription an hour earlier if anyone bothered paying attention to me. Instead, the time lapse has allowed her to potentially infect the entire room with her condition and I get to celebrate by continuing to sit in an uncomfortable wheelchair designed for someone twice my size.

Medical Observational Assessment – Continuous coughing indicates irritating inflammation of the throat, phlegm build-up and dry mouth. Water, red eyes and used tissues falling out of her purse suggest the cold has peaked and is most likely bordering the flu the way the woman's arms slowly began hugging her own body. Treatment – general paracetamol medication, sleep, constant fluids to flush system; hot/cold press against neck and temple to bring the body temperature down from a hovering 38 degrees. Recovery time – anywhere from five days to two weeks. Number of community members infected – probably hundreds.

So much for that initial call to have the staff prep for my arrival and expedite the process for one of their very own. Does being a doctor not mean anything to anyone around here?

Roughly two hours later, a nurse finally comes to take my blood pressure and document my injury story.

"You're in the wrong place," she states. "You should be in the Urgent Care unit."

No kidding! Seriously! I replied

"I'll have someone take you over there now."

I should have been relieved that someone finally acknowledged my existence but another hour waiting in Urgent Care erased any appreciation I might have felt for the attending staff. And, you'd think that with all the money filtering through a hospital, they could afford to liven up this place with more interesting photos on the walls or at least putting a channel on the television worth watching. The depressing news channel just wasn't doing it for me.

I tried to convince myself that I would never treat patients as poorly as I was being treated, but there was a small part of me that had a gut wrenching feeling that I already had. I was getting my first taste of what life was like from the patient perspective and I didn't like it, to say the least. Entering through the back door of the hospital was much easier than entering through the front. No one listened to me on this end.

4 The Diagnosis

The legends often told of the waiting rooms are all true. The lack of quality entertainment on the generic hospital walls makes you keenly aware of the eternity you're spending in a wildly uncomfortable chair and your waiting companions silently judge how severe your condition is to justify why they believe they should be seen before you.

I look down at my watch to verify what an eternity looks like. I was about to hit the four-hour mark. As much fun as the waiting room was turning out to be, it was time to get out of here. Someone better come get me quick before this hospital gets fined for breaching a government regulated policy. I'm technically supposed to be out of here in less than one hour.

I begin chuckling at my own thought process. One of the downsides to having free healthcare is that the NHS implements conflicting policies that ensure nothing except hospital fines. In this case, they wished to improve the quality of customer care by decreasing the time patients must wait to be seen, diagnosed, treated and exit the hospital doors. Patients should take no more than four hours from beginning to end. The thought behind the regulation comes from a good place but it doesn't exactly work. Even I could admit that this could have potentially been a great stride to help improve standards of healthcare except that it was countered with hefty budget cuts. That means less personnel to see, diagnose and treat the consistent influx of patients and this made reaching the targets set almost impossible to achieve.

Every time a patient is considered breached, the hospital is hit with a substantial fine. It's like a mathematician believing one plus two equals 47 or an alchemist who's still trying to make gold out of lead. They keep expecting quiche to come out of the oven when they're only using pancake ingredients. Money is being siphoned out of the hospitals through regulations. For what purpose? Not many know. I haven't met a single doctor who hasn't breached this hospital policy a handful of times, including myself. Not on purpose, of course. Doctors can be amazing people but they can't pull rabbits out of a hat.

All the staff members passing through the waiting room are avoiding eye contact with me. They conveniently look down at a clipboard filled with medical notes. Or, was it the latest newspaper crossword puzzle? Either way, they are on a mission that doesn't involve me.

Wait a moment. Who was this woman holding her gaze with mine? I think I know her. An X-ray technician! Bingo!

"Doctor? What are you doing in the waiting room?" she asks, clearly surprised to see me in this context.

"Sporting accident. Think I broke something in my leg." I reply. "No doctor had seen me yet and I have been waiting for nearly four hours, would you be willing to take some X-rays for me, please?"

"Sure. That's definitely something I can do," she answers, hurrying off.

Within a few moments, she had spoken about my request with the doctor and wheeled me in herself to begin taking a picture of my ankle.

"Would you take a photo of my entire leg?" I request.

"Oh, that's not what the doctor wanted," she hesitates.

"Trust me. When the Doc finds out that the pain runs up to my knee, he's going to want to see if I've fractured anything above the ankle as well. I'm just trying to save you time because I can guarantee he'll have you bring me right back here again later."

Taking a moment to think about it, she was convinced and snapped another photo surrounding the knee. Immediately, she could see how apparent the damage was.

"You were right! There's no question that the injury extends up your leg," she remarks.

Wow. This employee could take direction better than any professional I had run into so far. What a relief. Sort of. I was secretly hoping I was wrong about the multiple fractures. Either way, I felt the need to keep this worker close by just in case I needed anything else.

I heard my mobile phone ringing again. That would be my parents doing their part to keep me as close to them as the distance between us would allow. However, I had nothing new to tell, so I was hesitant to answer. They keep asking all the questions I still have yet to ask the orthopaedic doctor.

"Yes, Mum," I acquiesced. "Some fractures can heal comfortably without surgery and other times surgery is a requirement. I honestly don't know what else to tell you. I haven't seen the doctor yet."

Calling, texting, emailing, video chatting. There are so many communication methods at our disposal but there is no communication actually happening with the one person I need the most. If only I had this mysterious doctor on speed dial.

My excitement peaks as a physician finally walks in.

"I'm not your doctor," he states.

False alarm. I didn't bother disguising the disappointment on my face.

"I'm the junior doctor assisting the orthopaedic surgeon who will be coming to speak with you about your X-rays after he finishes a surgery. In the meantime, a cast has been ordered for you."

As if on cue, several nurses walk in behind him. While the older, more experienced one draws my blood, the two younger ones hesitantly move about the room with timid apprehension. Their youthfulness was a tad disconcerting.

"We're going to be putting the cast all the way up above your knee…"

No, seriously. How old are you?

"So, we need you to take your pants off."

Seventeen? Eighteen? How are you enjoying high school? Oh, dear me. Good thing this head nurse is here to make sure they know what they're doing. A full leg cast seems a little over the top but I do as I'm told to help move things along.

An hour later, like delayed clockwork, the orthopaedic surgeon arrives (so he *does* exist!) and apologises for the wait.

"So, I hear you've had a nasty fall on the ice. I've looked over your X-rays and I'm going to get right down to it." His brisk and efficient manner was reassuring. Finally! This was someone I could get on board with. I was growing increasingly agitated with insincere apologies about my wasted time. I'm a "get on with it, get to the point" kind of person. It's like when a friend or family member calls to tell you a story and goes on and on when all you're really interested in is the final resolve, the conclusion, that "ta-da" moment. Here was my "ta-da" moment. This guy had some useful information for me and I'll take it! Or, at least that's how I felt before he ripped the bandage off my rising emotions and exposed my situation for what it really was.

I held my breath through his entire assessment as a flood of helplessness overwhelmed my psyche. My ankle truly was fractured in two different places including severe damage to the surrounding ligaments. Surgery would be required to properly set the bone with screws.

I desperately wanted to advise he take another look at the X-rays, but stirring the medical pot by desperately searching for a differential diagnosis would be a worthless endeavour. Begging a doctor for his professional opinion and then questioning his diagnosis usually proves futile like it probably had for almost every other patient before me.

"We can probably schedule your surgery to be done in about a week to allow the swelling in your leg to go down. After we take another X-ray to make sure the cast is supporting your ankle properly, there's no reason why you can't go home tonight." His speech slows as he looks down inquisitively at my bandaged leg. "Why did they give you a full leg cast?" he asks rhetorically, shaking his head in disapproval. "That was unnecessary."

Yeah. I liked this guy. Maybe it was the fact that we seemed to be like-minded professionals or it could have been because he had the power to finally let me go home. Either way, I was relieved he would be the one overseeing this operation rather than the children who put on this ginormous cast.

One more stop and then I was home free! It was getting late into the evening which meant that I would have been starting my night shift on-call at my own hospital if the events of the last 12 hours had not broken my spirit in addition to my body. The thought of sleeping on my own pillow, in my own bed and in my own flat put the biggest smile on my face.

Wheeling down the hallway to visit the X-ray technician, the junior doctor from earlier stops me midway to deliver an unexpected message.

"Change of plans," he states cheerfully. "We're going to do the operation tomorrow. Looks like you'll be sleeping here tonight."

5 The Admission

Nooo! I was so close. I could feel the exit doors of the hospital beckoning me towards the sweet smell of London's fresh, smoggy air and away from the stench of my own helplessness. Forget Murphy's Law. It felt like Sod's law was well under way as I was finishing a CT scan in preparation for surgery the next day. Not only will I not get to sleep in my own bed, but I have to eat hospital food.

I'm wheeled into the elevator and watch each level light up as we pass – four, five, six. A few more dings and we would be on the ninth floor. Out of all the patient wards in this entire hospital, how was it that the only room they had available was on the very unit I had worked with the staff to complete my specialty training.

When I first showed up to the hospital, Uber in tow, my eyes were desperately searching for someone I knew who could expedite my hospital visit. I had purposely come to one of the top university hospitals in the world and knew I could count on them to treat me well and provide me with the best possible care. However, I hadn't thought this far ahead and things were different now. I had officially been diagnosed. It was documented that I was weak, dependent on others and needed to be taken care of round the clock. I was to be directed by others rather than me directing them. I wasn't calling the shots anymore. Someone else was now in charge.

I knew the majority of the people on this unit. I had instructed nurses, overseen resident doctors and advised patients. Now the juniors who used to train under me would no longer be looking up to me as a doctor but down at me as a helpless patient who couldn't even take an elevator ride without an escort.

I begin fidgeting at the thought of everyone putting me under a microscope as the newest focus of their attention. I was more out of my element than I was comfortable admitting. I tugged lightly at my hospital wristband to see how difficult it would be to take off. As long as I had this thing on, I had no control.

The elevator doors open and the lack activity and pitter-patter of professional feet remind me of the late hour. I may not end up seeing as many people tonight as I thought. I'd wait to be embarrassed when more people are running around tomorrow morning.

My eyes grow heavier as the evening passes on. Not an unusual feeling for a doctor on the night shift but as a patient, I was allowed to give in.

"Am I going to be in a private, side room?" I asked my escort, hoping to enjoy some perks of being a doctor.

"No. I'm afraid you'll have a few roommates for the night."

Never mind. I recant my last thought. There doesn't seem to be any perks of being a doctor after all except that I may know my way around the hospital more than a typical patient might. I don't know why I keep settling on the idea that I'll be treated differently than anyone else. Sure, I would have preferred the privacy of my own room but even when I'm working, doctors are often passed out in the busy staff lounges during their breaks. I should not have asked for special treatment. I'm too tired to care now anyway. Just don't put me next to an infectious cougher. I had already had my fill of that in the waiting room.

Entering the patient room, the nurses are busy going about their routine, seemingly unprepared for my arrival. This was understandable since I only found out myself a few moments prior that I'd be spending the night. They were sanitising the area, preparing the bedding, checking my blood pressure, preparing the drip…

"Oh, don't bother putting in a drip until morning. No one drinks while they're asleep anyway," I said to the nurse, just wanting to get in to bed.

"No problem," the nurse assents.

As I watch them finish up, my thoughts drift off with a more melancholy tone. The staff on this ward have probably seen hundreds, probably thousands of patients just like me come through their doors. Every single day, they assist people just like me on their path to becoming physically whole again so they can discharge them back out into the world.

I force my thoughts to pause before mustering up the courage to acknowledge an unavoidable reality. Sure, there were people who got well again, but there were also a few who didn't. No doubt the staff here had seen that, too. What if I turned out to be one of those patients who couldn't be helped? What if the damage to my leg was so severe that I could no longer walk? What if I could no longer practice medicine? What career path could I fall back on?

Shaking my head, I scold myself for entertaining so much irrationality. Of course, I could still practice medicine. And, I wouldn't need a wheelchair because these kinds of accidents don't typically cause permanent damage. It certainly didn't take long for my thoughts to get the best of me but I could easily blame it on the late hour.

At 2 a.m., I'm jerked awake by a lingering thought that I forgot to do something. Actually, *they* forgot to do something. I'm supposed to have an anti-clot injection. I call for the nurse.

"No. They don't want you to have one tonight," a nurse comes in to confirm.

"Alright.   Thank you," I hesitate, rather puzzled.

That's odd. I was sure the doctor had ordered me one, but I suppose the nurses on duty would know what final orders were given. Plus, I didn't want to be labelled a problem patient like the guy next to me. He was obnoxiously noisy and didn't seem as trusting of the system as I was. The staff was responding to his call every few minutes to let him know that everything was alright and re-explaining their answers to the same questions he had already asked two or three times before that. No, he wasn't delusional, but I wouldn't put it past the staff to joke about it in the back.

I finally drift off back to sleep around three or four in the morning. I wasn't sure but it didn't matter. Before I became a doctor, it was difficult to fall asleep somewhere other than my own bed. The comforts of home could not be easily replaced but medical school changes the need for that. You spend so much of your time improving your experience and knowledge to keep up with your medical surroundings that you forget to focus on your basic needs. Pushing yourself to the brink of exhaustion, almost any chair becomes suitable enough to sleep in.

6 The Surgery

I wake up to my paranoid neighbour ordering breakfast – two eggs with no salt and toast. The cook also needs to put on new gloves when preparing the food because otherwise he won't eat any of it. As for the coffee, the staff better not forget his cup like they had so many times before.

Honestly, how long had this guy been here? His noisy presence is a clear reminder that my accident on the ice was not a dream like I was hoping it would turn out to be. The cast weighing down my lower body and limiting my mobility was an unwelcome symbol of my pain. I really had hurt myself. I really did trade an ambulance ride for an Uber. And, the clock on the wall tells me that I really was going to have surgery within a few hours. I go to tug lightly at my hospital wrist band again.

Sitting up in bed, I smile at a few recognisable faces and my old colleague, Nurse Katie, comes over to check my blood pressure and fill me in on why I didn't receive my anti-clot injection. Apparently, the doctor had ordered me one like I originally thought but he failed to identify a specific time to administer it, so they didn't honour the prescription. I was floored and Katie would get a clear reading of my irritation.

"I can see I should have told you this information *after* I took your blood pressure," she smirks.

"That's outrageous!" I yell as loud as my paranoid neighbour. "Did they even bother checking with my doctor?"

"I'm not sure," she replies, looking rather dismal.

"A blood clot isn't what we'd call a joke when it teases the issue of crippling a patient. Stopping blood flow. How is that a good thing?! Has management begun filling this ward with locum staff?!" Furious, I begin to try moving my toes and flexing my calf muscle under my cast to keep the blood circulating... just in case.

"You know you can file a complaint if you want to," Katie suggests.

The thought of requesting an incident form was almost embarrassing. I knew how much of a time waster it was for almost everyone involved. Sure, I've personally witnessed colleagues get a slap on the wrist from superiors sifting through their patient complaints, but how much of a difference is that going to make in their long-term behaviour anyway? Very few people take those seriously.

I rolled my eyes. "No disrespect but does anyone even look at those?"

The tone of employee behaviour was different than what I remember as a doctor here. Hospital administrations are growing fond of filling their floors with temporary staff rather than full-time employees. The advantages of having employees on a short-term contract typically have to do with their financial bottom line. Simply put, the hospital saves money, paying less overall for a professional's temporary stay. The pressure from the government to save money is so severe that I think even general staff training has become a target of budget cuts.

The disadvantages of hiring temporary staff, however, significantly outweigh the advantages, and my situation would be a perfect example. Instead of having a staff that has learned how to work with one another, they are replaced with temporary, mediocre, or second-string (often cheaper) picks who have no motivation to establish rapport and a positive working relationship with the other professionals around them. After all, what's the point when they will most likely not be working there within the next few months. So, they shoulder less responsibilities and sideline important tasks like investing themselves in patient concerns, going the extra mile or simply confirming an anti-clot injection.

Patient safety proves to be the biggest problem of all. The shorter time a physician spends at a hospital, the less he or she has interacted with their patients and the less they understand their patient's histories and personal concerns. And with the 4-hour control addendum hovering over their shoulder and limiting their quality of service, patients are pushed out with recommendations very often not suitable for their conditions. I thought this hospital was above jumping on the bank and locum staffing bandwagon but perhaps they're feeling the pressure from government to save money the same way everyone else seems to be.

The details of their incompetence interested me greatly considering these were the professionals assigned to care for me. Things were worse than I thought. Not only do you not get special treatment as a doctor, you don't even get the *prescribed* treatment!

"There really is no excuse for that, especially since it's so easy to pick up the phone to confirm a prescription with a doctor," she acknowledges my angst.

Her bedside manner was impeccable. "You're one of the good ones, Katie."

Once again, I've never been much of a complainer. It reminds me too much of the on-going, time-wasting battle between nurses and doctors that I try desperately to avoid because the complaining has more to do with hurt feelings rather than the care and safety of a patient. The concentration shifts from the importance of patient wellness to the unimportant professional emotions and bravado.

"Whoever writes the first email wins!" one of my superiors once told me. It's a sad reality. Since most doctors are too busy making patient notes mid-rounds to do anything else, they usually lose out. As the end of their workday comes to a close, they open their email only to find their inbox overflowing with passive confrontations regarding personal issues that have already been well-circulated amongst the management staff. Now you've got more than one person upset that you haven't responded in a "timely manner" despite the fact that your time has been spent on the biggest priority of all – patient care. Thankfully, the floor managers stop us from grabbing scalpels and settling these issues like medical professionals.

Now I'm a patient failing to receive optimal care by the very people I used to work with. Instead, I get a passing nod while my neighbour, Mr. Paranoia, in the next bed gets all the attention. I feel like I've been let down by the very people I used to work with. Why do loud people always get what they want? Perhaps I was wrong and there's more I can learn from this guy than he could learn from me.

I expected a team of doctors to come around eight in the morning but found only Angela, the floor anaesthetist, approaching my bedside.

"Hey, Yahya! Good morning. I was surprised to see your name on my list today," she laughed.

"Ah, my favourite drug pusher. You must be here to talk to me about how you're going to pump me full of glorious narcotics." It was nice to see another familiar face.

"Yes, sir. So, what are you thinking? Would you prefer general anaesthesia or spinal?" she asked.

Not expecting an option, I was stumped. I certainly would not have given any of my patients a choice on the matter. I contemplated the idea of being awake during the surgery, overseeing the process and holding on to what little control I had left. But, honestly, who was I kidding? I had lost control the moment I was pushed through the hospital's doors in a wheelchair.

"I'll take general anaesthesia," I reply, relinquishing the last bit of control. After all, I wouldn't have suggested spinal to the majority of my patients because unanticipated body movements that often come with being awake can impede the surgeon's ability to work. Plus, I knew there would be a lot of chatter in the surgery room amongst the staff and not all of it is medically related. Doctors talk a lot, we laugh with one another, we crack jokes and we often tease scrub nurses. I knew it would be best I disconnected myself from the conversation altogether. I'd avoid the pain of a needle in my back and accept the general anaesthesia.

"Good decision!" My doctor chimed in. Him and his team of trainees had crept up on us. I had fully expected his posse of clones since that's how the daily rounds around the ward were usually conducted at a teaching hospital. But, no matter how familiar I was with how things were done in groups, I was unnerved to have so many pairs of eyes staring down at me.

"I understand that you're a serious skater," the doctor acknowledges.

I could see the cause of my injury came up in their morning doctors' meeting. I hope they weren't expecting a demonstration.

"We've looked at the X-rays and CT scan," he continues, "and we'll need to put screws in your ankle to help align the bone. The ligament in your upper leg has also been torn which makes the leg even more unstable. Those are the basics but we'll know the full extent of the damage as soon as we're able to take a look on the inside."

"How long will the recovery process take before I can begin skating again?" I ask, nervous for the true response.

"Roughly three months, give or take. My colleague here is going to run you through the consent paperwork you'll need to sign before we roll you into surgery within the next hour." He moved off to the next patient before I had a chance to digest the information provided.

My orthopaedic surgeon was so professional and I had full trust in him. He was in and out in less than ten minutes and already had his paper-pusher repeating all the legal, medical disclaimers to me: the surgery may not work, I may get an infection, additional surgeries may be required and the list goes on.

I looked at the young chap reading through his notes. How many times had I given the worst case scenario speech to others? *I'm* not supposed to be hearing this from someone else. I'm supposed to be *giving* it. Although, to be fair, I could tell the junior doctor enjoyed this task as much as I enjoyed hearing it. It's never easy to come up with an elegant way of informing a patient, "Hey, something crazy could happen during surgery and you could die." I quickly signed the boy's legal paperwork, relieving him of his duty.

My world was still backwards and this change was growing increasingly uncomfortable as I sat waiting for someone to cut me open. All those medical disclaimers were no longer a minor side note. These issues were dangerous and staring me right in the face. They weren't about someone else. They were directed at me.

I'd given that speech a million times myself so why was I so shaken? Why was I distracted by all the "what if" scenarios running through my mind? I'm a doctor. I'm a professional. I know better than to be giving so much weight on the smallest of chances something horrible would happen to me. But, as irrational as it may be, the small risk had my heart racing.

A nurse came to distract my concerns with her pre-surgery checklist. Did I have any allergies? Did I change into a hospital gown? Did I remove my underwear?

Wait a second. My underwear? Why would I need to remove those if they were only operating on my leg?

"If you don't remove them, they may end up doing it for you," she states.

"Look," I respond. "I'm a surgeon. They're not operating on my rectum, thank goodness. So, if

73

they don't need access to that area, I'll just keep them on."

"Alright, then," she smiles sweetly. "We'll be going to the operating theatre shortly."

By shortly, she meant almost two hours later. As I was wheeled in bed down the corridor, I see a few more familiar faces. Some old colleagues instructing their juniors and nurses going to and fro. I was annoyed that my bed seemed to have more control than I did, pushing the corridor's double doors open with little effort and forcing staff members to move aside. I knew I was eventually going to have to give up on this line of thinking, that control was something I still possessed. Now was as good a time as any to put my full trust in the people about to operate on me.

Easier said than done.

The elevator closes us in and the numbers begin counting down as if it knew where it was taking me. It releases me on the third floor and we glide down a hallway so long that the anaesthetist's assistant has time to converse and makes jokes with me.

"Don't worry, man. We'll be good to you. We won't torture you as much as we do the others." He's joking right. Medical professionals can joke. That's normal.

I'm wheeled into the anaesthesia room, a place I wish we could get rid of all together.

Last year I had the opportunity to spend time in the United States on a fellowship program, during which I was able to observe and appreciate the practicality of patients going straight into the operating theatre because it decreased the transition time. However, it's kept here so that many patients (especially young ones) can enjoy comfort of being with a family member as we put them to sleep. Thousands of patients before me were able to squeeze the hand of a loved one close by or listen as a prayer was whispered in their ear. Unlike them, I had no such companion nearby. In a place where I would have no control over my destiny, my outcome, there was one last entity I could seek help from. Being Muslim, I whispered a prayer to myself in Arabic that roughly translates to, "God is the best guardian and He is the most merciful of the merciful." I had done all I could do. Now, I just had to wait.

I looked at my old colleagues, busy about the room, finishing their surgery preparations. I was usually part of this medical hive of activity. There were a few moments when I was sure they had forgotten I was in the room, but I appreciate their focus. I knew the mental checklists that were going through their heads.

Medical Observational Assessment: Confirm patient identity – name, hospital ID number, date of birth. Prepare oxygen mask. Confirm machines are calibrated correctly. Prepare IV for anaesthesia. Time until drugs take effect – roughly 10-30 seconds.

"We're going to give you the anaesthesia now," the doctor says. "So, think of something nice. Imagine yourself sunbathing on a nice beach or that double axel you'll be able to do on the ice soon."

As of this moment, the thought of drugs pumping through my system fascinated me more than anything else and I wondered how quickly my body would begin to feel it. His words were comforting, though. These professionals were optimistic that I'd be able to continue my sporting adventures. They are right. One day I would be able to perform that single and double axel. I'll be amazing. I'll be a pro. I'll be …

Zzzzzz.

7 The Recovery Room

Once again, I wake up to the standard hospital noises of blood pressure and IV fluid machines in full swing but this time they're muffled behind a beige curtain that's providing me with some limited privacy. All the background chatter indicates the surgical recovery room is just as full as the rest of the hospital wards.

I wondered how many people had to spend the night here in the recovery bay because the wards were completely full with new patients. The doctor side of me is tempted to calculate how many scheduled surgeries would potentially have to be cancelled if no room was available while the patient side of me was too grateful with my own bed to care.

Finding an empty hospital bed is rare, after all, which is why having a scheduled appointment is so important. However, that often won't stop a hospital from sending a patient elsewhere or rescheduling them last minute because something of a higher priority is now taking precedence like a possible breech (financial penalty) with another non-emergency elective patient. So, there's a high chance that if other patients had to spend the night in this surgical recovery ward even though they were cleared to go the ward. Other people waiting weeks or maybe months for a much needed surgery would be greeted with a "No Vacancy" sign right beside the hospital's "Welcome" entrance.

It's easy and completely understandable to be horrified by this concept. Nobody likes the idea of sending people away from a hospital, not doctors and especially not patients. From a management perspective, if large amounts of money are taken away from the budgets to pay government regulated fines, then there's less money to allocate for updated medical equipment and staffing salaries. So, the downward spiral continues as an understaffed hospital attempts to treat the same number of patients with older, broken down equipment.

Under the current regulations and targets, the simplest answer may be to discharge healthy patients from the medical wards. This may seem like an obvious point to make but attempting to discharge patients is a battle all in its own when a free healthcare system gives much of the power to the patients who find it irresistibly tempting to milk the system for as long as possible, extending their stay longer than is necessary. It's equivalent to a homeless person pretending that something is physically wrong so they can receive full service meals complete with a bed for sleeping. These issues tug at the heartstrings as well as the hospital's wallet.

If a patient asks for something that a doctor cannot fulfill (like treating them for something they don't actually have), the extreme walk-ins will begin fabricating something else in its place which prolongs their hospital stay. I've personally witnessed three patients in a ward who stayed for a combined total of two years. Trying to discharge them only led to increased complaints that were filed against the staff, such as:

"The doctor was mean to me and didn't test me for what I came in for."

"The nurses were uncooperative in addressing my needs."

"I'm displeased with the service provided because I did not get the medication that I wanted."

When the system works against doctors like this, most of them do one of three things:

One, they do what's right for the public and discharge a healthy patient which makes a bed available for someone who really needs it but they knowingly accept the unfortunate repercussions of patient complaints about their 'unprofessional' behaviour. This wouldn't normally be a big deal but these complaints are time consuming to address.

The second option is to cater to every whimsical need of a patient. Does a patient refuse to go home and demands continued monitoring? It's easy to see why some physicians just walk away to attend to their other patients then embrace the backlash that will come with complaints.

The third option doctors have in response to a working environment they can't get on board with is to simply leave. It's commonly known as reverse immigration where the best professionals are choosing to leave the country altogether in search of a medical community that maintains higher standards of care than subject themselves to flaws found within socialized medicine. In turn, the NHS system is being flooded with semi-qualified professionals, second string players from all around the world to fill the vacant positions of those leaving. Or, to be more generous, they are fully qualified elsewhere, but don't know the ropes at these hospitals. Although, I suppose all professionals are only as good as their training.

A nurse in the recovery bay catches my eye through a gap left between the curtains and comes over to check on me. He updates me on the success of the surgery and asks if I want anything to eat. Too groggy to respond verbally, I decline with a loose gesture of my hand. My hands instinctively start looking for my chart notes as if I'm on duty. I may only be semi-conscious but I wouldn't waste any more time figuring out what they had done to me. I ask the nurse to read the operation notes out loud as I listen with eyes half closed.

"Small lateral incision. Dissection down to bone. Exposure through AITFL / anterior to fibula. Fibula reduced into notch and stabilized with tenaculum with foot in plantigrade (NB tight TA on right ankle with foot only to PG). 2mm Kwire to confirm drill path. x2 fully threated cortical positional screws inserted and fully tapped. Satisfactory. Small posterior fragment comminuted on CT and not explored."

Unsure of how to proceed, the nurse offers food once more.

"A Kit Kat," I chuckle, knowing they would never have that available. What can I say? I had a craving.

Wait a second. Forget the snacks. A breeze snuck under my bed sheets and had me feeling uncomfortably exposed all of a sudden. Where is my underwear? The nurse points to a clear bag beside my bed. That nurse in the ward was true to her word when she said what would happen if I didn't submit them willingly before the surgery. I suppose I had been warned.

As the evening shift begins, I'm cleared to make a trip back to the ninth floor ward, and it turns into a little adventure as I begin waving at everyone I know like a pageant girl who doesn't know she's been drugged up by another contestant. They all greet me kindly including an attractive brunette finishing her rounds.

"Hello, there! Are you Sophie?" I ask, cheerfully.

"Hi," the woman looks at me confused. "Do you know me?"

"Yeah! Of course, I know you."

"Wow. Alright," she laughs at my lack of filter.

"I'm a doctor, too! I'll be in bed 54. Come visit me," I tease. Clearly, I was in a strange mood.

The floor nurses welcome me back and get me settled into my cove before checking my pulse.

Medical Observational Assessment: High pulse between 102-110 elevated from an average 65. Pupils dilated. Increased verbal engagement and clarity of thought proven through responsiveness to questions. All details indicate full recovery is well under way.

In other words, I'm still high with residual amounts of anaesthesia in my system. Thankfully, nobody seemed to mind my gleeful disposition.

I look down relieved to find I only had a half-leg cast on rather than a full, unnecessary one. They did it properly this time.

A coffee and sandwich are delivered the same time the brunette doctor stops in for a visit.

"Hiiiii!" I dramatically greet her smiling.

It was nice to have a visitor even though I only knew her by association, explaining that I worked with her sister in another hospital. Having some company turned out to be more enjoyable than I expected. With her shift completed for the day, we chatted for well over an hour. I welcomed her empathetic bedside manner and we continued chatting about the need for a better work/life balance. She helped me forget how bored and, more importantly, alone I felt prior to the surgery.

"How's your family dealing with your accident? Are they calling your phone every few minutes?" she asked. We both laugh as I pick up my vibrating mobile from the side table.

"They keep wanting to know specific details about my foot but I have to remind them that I'm not an orthopaedic surgeon. They just assume that I'm comfortable talking specifics about an area that is not my specialty. Story of our life, right?"

Specialty or not, my doctor alter-ego was coming back to life as the anaesthesia wore off and I had successfully got my hands on my X-rays and operation notes because I couldn't remember anything the nurse read to me when I first woke up in the recovery bay. Most patients wouldn't ask to see the X-rays or the operation note but most patients aren't doctors either. I *need* to see them. I probably wouldn't be so antsy if they hadn't put foreign objects in my body. I needed all my questions answered right now.

My general concerns were minimized knowing that my doctor didn't have my scans outsourced to be read and interpreted by someone outside the local system. He had personally reviewed them and made his own recommendations. Outsourcing isn't just a popular concept in the retail industry where companies have hundreds of manufacturing plants outside their country or in phone companies, who have been known to outsource services to outside entities. I can't remember the number of times I've called a help line and it routed me to someone I could barely understand.

The medical industry is falling in line when it comes to the importance of saving money. Rather than budgeting salaries to maintain full-time radiologists, many hospitals are sending electronic copies of X-rays and CT scans to specialists in other countries like Australia and India, who then interpret and provide their own recommendations.

The roadblock occurs when your doctor disagrees with the diagnosis and/or recommendation and they aren't given the opportunity to converse with the individual overseas who originally read the images because the contracts are set up in a way that only allows for one time, one-way communication. Images are sent and recommendations are received. The process is quick and easy but potentially harmful to patients.

I've received recommendations from outside countries on the treatment of my own patients that have turned out to be blatantly incorrect. Uncomfortable taking the recommendations of someone I haven't had the opportunity to work with personally, I double-check the analysis and often override the original treatment plans for the sake of my patient's health and safety.

With the option of outsourcing as a convenient crutch, local radiologists who are paid to be on call 24/7 often refuse to answer the late evening calls, opting to push the responsibility of reading images to someone else outside the country. Furthermore, the more pressure hospitals receive to cut costs, the more outsourcing we're likely to see in the future. I considered myself lucky to be under the supervision of a doctor who took the time to fully assess my situation themselves rather than relying on others to do it for them.

8 Discharged

If somebody put crutches by my hospital bed at this very moment, I wouldn't know what I was doing. As a doctor, the oddity of that confession does not escape me. It's just one of those fluke things, I suppose. The fact that I managed to grow up male without making one catastrophic visit to the emergency room is almost unheard of since most boys are prone to bone crushing adventures of some sort or another.

Then there comes my formal education. There was no class in medical school called "Crutches – The Post Surgical Balancing Act" that had us manoeuvring from room to room like a disabled conga line. That's why I was pleased my doctor scheduled me for a session with the hospital's physiotherapist who would show me the ropes. Sadly, it turned out to be more of a 15-minute meet-and-greet rather than learning anything useful. She had me go up and down a few steps in the stairway but that was pretty much it. Walking on flat ground didn't seem to be on the schedule so I didn't get a chance to practice. Perhaps they didn't feel the need to because London's streets are so wildly uneven. Or worse, this could be the accepted standard for how things should always be done with patients.

"My steps at home are much narrower than these. Is that going to be a problem?" This was completely new territory for me so my questions were limited. First timers rarely know what they should be asking. I had never been broken like this before. Not to mention, I was too busy trying to steady my balance and not hurt myself again to think of more quality questions.

"No. It'll be fine," the therapist reassures me.

Clearly, our communication was deeply constructive. I guess all my in-depth conversations were used up yesterday when a couple of friends trickled in one-by-one to make sure I was still alive. After the friendly doctor sat with me for much longer than expected (I'm assuming she was entertained by my drugged-up demeanour like so many others were), my friend George called and kindly took my order for a Diet Coke and Kit Kat only to show up with a non-diet beverage and Oreos. Like I mentioned earlier, I'm not big on complaining, but when a grown man asks for something as seemingly insignificant as a Kit Kat, he's definitely not joking around. I had slightly better luck when my friend Yasmin who brought my soda and some fruit.

Having a few friends by my side filled an unexpected void of belonging. With me feeling out of my element in my own work environment, forced to take a back seat in the day to day routine, the detachment had me missing human interaction on the most basic levels. I had even begun to grow fond of my neighbour's ranting but the nursing staff was too annoyed to laugh with me. So, when my friends came by, I was thrilled to share the humour with my visitors who didn't hesitate to stir the pot of his paranoia.

Looking down at my phone, I see a handful of unread messages from other people wanting to check up on me—a few friends and my parents again. Thankfully, no crying this time around. I wasn't sure how much more of that I could take. But, no matter. I was already on the mend and would be leaving the hospital soon to go back to my own home where I could freely relax without more residents putting me under the microscope.

Shortly after the morning's physiotherapy session, my nurse gave me the option of waiting in my bed rather than the noisy discharge lounge for departure. How thoughtful of him. I certainly did not want to sit around in that fish market again after the extensive waiting I had already done upon my arrival. Why would I go out there with all those people when I could just stay here where it's much more comfortable? I could definitely see how a patient wouldn't want to leave their bed once they've secured one. Plus, I could avoid falling on my face in front of my colleagues when attempting to use my new crutches.

Around noon, my doctor offers me a consolation prize for my participation of enduring my first major surgery—pain killers. I didn't want to leave the party without a goody bag just in case I had trouble sleeping the first few nights, so I accepted. But, over an hour later, the pharmacist stops by and sees that I haven't received any medication, so off she runs to expedite that for me.

Seven o'clock rolls around and I'm beginning to think they've forgotten about me. It's difficult not to feel that way when discharge procedures began after my physiotherapy session around 11 a.m. I would discharge myself but I'm not sure if these professionals have any closing instructions before I frolic off to reclaim my independence.

I finally make it outside as the sun departs ahead of me, hints of a sunset still peeking over the horizon. The light from inside an ambulance guides me in to a seat beside two other patients being taxied home, goody bags in hand. I immediately regret allowing my day to be completely wasted. I could have easily and more conveniently had an Uber take me directly home.

Trying to avoid any detours, I somehow convinced the driver to take me home first. It took about 10 minutes to exit the actual hospital itself premises, as if the driver was convinced he had unprotected, porcelain delicates laying around in the back. I may have struggled and needed assistance to crawl into the vehicle, but I was not delicate! I needed the driver to start pressing that accelerator. Time was of the essence.

Why was it that every environment I found myself in since the accident seemed to work in slow motion? The drive to the hospital, the waiting rooms, the CT scan results, honouring drug prescriptions, the discharge process. It's like the universe was trying to send me an important message about the pace of life I should be embracing. Even the night-time roads we drove on seemed to agree. A few, scattered street lights illuminated the walkways and noted a few people strolling around. No one seemed to be in a rush. Everything seemed at ease. It was a pace of life I'd been trying to avoid. However, now I wasn't sure if it was because I didn't have time to relax or if I didn't *make* the time.

For me, getting from point A to point B in the shortest period of time is the key to a successful day. Quick pace was the name of the daily game. But, not as of late. If I had an award for the fastest emergency responder through this experience so far, it would inevitably go to the nurse who came out yelling at my driver for parking in the ambulance bay. Runner up would have to be the driver himself. Although, I think his motivation to get me to the hospital quickly had less to do with my pain and a bit more to do with getting me out of his vehicle as soon as possible to save himself from additional mental anguish.

Three flights of narrow stairs were ready to greet me when I got to my apartment building. With no railing to hold onto, I had to sit on each step and use my arms to lift myself up backwards. Concerned, the ambulance driver patiently held my belongings while I climbed up myself.

"This, really, is not ok. They should have sent another person to assist you. Did you tell them how narrow your stairs are?"

"I did," I replied, struggling up another step.

"Why didn't they listen?" he persisted.

"I don't know."

I hesitated before beginning the third flight of stairs, catching my breath and hoping he wouldn't probe about anything else further. There were turning out to be a lot of things done by professionals during my hospital stay that I could not understand. Not being able to explain the actions of my own people was unnerving to say the least. Why did every medical task take so long? Why did the noisy patients get all the speedy attention? Why was my time with the physiotherapist not more thorough? And, why, for the love of everything holy, couldn't my apartment be on the first floor?!

9 Home Again

Realising I left the bedroom light on, I reach for my crutches leaning up against the end of the couch and hobble back over to turn it off. Normally, the lights wouldn't bother me, but I was trying to make up for those three days I was unexpectedly delayed in turning them off. Not to mention, I left the heater on full blast, too. So, I wasn't looking forward to my next electricity and heating bill.

I released my hand from one crutch to flip the switch. I had been home for a couple weeks now and was becoming substantially more skilled at using crutches compared to the first few days. Basic tasks like making coffee and using the bathroom (essentials to living) were no longer an issue. Maintaining one's sanity with productivity, even at its most basic levels, is the wisdom I've managed to glean from this unwanted experience so far.

With the light now off, I cautiously pause outside my bedroom door as memories flash back to those unstable moments when I first came home from the hospital. The floor wasn't even slippery but attempting to multitask as a beginner had me flat on my bum in no time. Thankfully, nobody had been visiting me at the time to witness the incident, so the only person forcing me to relive the experience was myself.

Medical Observational Assessment: Localised sensitivity created by direct impact to the coccyx area. Temporary pain extending from the vertebral column. Severe damage to the surrounding joints and ligaments due to fall – unlikely. Chance of bruising – guaranteed, thanks to multiple falls. Slight emotional damage – more like extensive.

I glanced over to my pain pills sitting alone on my kitchen counter. Throughout this whole disastrous experience, I've only taken one Codeine pill that was offered moments after I arrived to the hospital. I have a high threshold for pain, so it was more of a courtesy "Welcome to the hospital!" token rather than a "Give me anything you've got so I can pretend like I'm not here" pill. I probably would not have been so quick to pop it if there had not been so many potholes on the way there.

My falls at home weren't fatal, but to make sure I wouldn't hurt myself again, Yasmin came over during my second day back to help prep me for a much needed shower. Knowing she was coming had my hyperosmia kicked into high gear and I was keenly aware of the smell not only protruding from a stack of dirty clothes on my bedroom floor and the overflowing trash pin in the kitchen, but from me specifically. I could more than just smell it, I could feel it. Perspiration on my face, clammy hands, the clear need for fresh deodorant. The hospital odour that followed me home was different than what I was accustomed to. Forced to live in my own filth, my hygiene took a backseat to my more immediate needs. Thankfully, Yasmin was a champ in not making it an issue even though she witnessed my self-neglect and unwillingness to shave the gorilla mask on my face. She wrapped a plastic bag around my cast and positioned a stool inside the shower that would allow me to reach everything I needed to.

Even though I was embarrassed at becoming so dependent on another person for such primitive tasks, I accepted her generosity without complaint. Plus, what is there to gripe about when a friend fills your refrigerator with loads of goodies including mandarins, milk and a huge bag of Kit Kat bars. Sure, they were all gone within 24 hours. But, if anyone asks, I'll confess to only one a day.

When I finally made it out of the shower, I found my apartment slightly cleaner than moments before. Women really are the best. Very often, they tend to pay better attention to those little details of life that help keep us functional. It's so easy to take all of that for granted when you're too busy focusing on bigger items

When my basic physiological and safety needs had been met and I wasn't going to scare away my neighbours (and their pets) with a deteriorating hygiene, my psychological needs were unavoidably staring me right in the face. I could eventually learn to physically adapt to a new way of functioning but how I *felt* about all this change was a completely different story and I avoided confronting the issue of my new lifestyle for as long as possible.

I found temporary solace in running Netflix nonstop until I ran out of documentaries and other historical shows. Don't they upload new episodes every day? The Discovery Channel doesn't just stop discovering, do they? Maybe running their programmes for so long ruined their system. Can you break Netflix?

Once again, I found myself flopped on my couch, left alone with my thoughts and staring up at my ceiling as if it could answer my one question that bothered my soul – What on earth am I supposed to do with myself now?

I truly believe that everything happens for a reason but I was having a difficult time figuring out what good could come from not being able to go to work and practice medicine. I had grown accustomed to a set schedule outlining my days but was now living minute by minute, questioning the laws of the universe, or more specifically, my life choices and where they had brought me.

I chose to study hard in my field so that I could work hard in my career, putting in the long hours now so I wouldn't have to later. Like so many others, I'm guilty of allowing moments of my work day to fill up with thoughts of what I could be doing elsewhere, dreaming a fun vacation here or there. But, before we even know what's happened, we're conditioned to live a life constantly on the move, unable to stop or finding it difficult to restructure our days. Now I have all the time in the world and I don't know what to do with it.

The thought of boredom terrified me so much that I grabbed a notepad from my desk and eagerly began scribbling down a few things I needed to accomplish, separating columns for priorities and just for fun. There were books I wanted to read, presents I needed to buy for the upcoming holidays and trips I'd been wanting to plan both local and far away; all designed to help me have a sense of accomplishment and provide purpose to my days. I'd been wanting to improve my Spanish fluency, learn to make more than just marmalade in the kitchen, learning how to play the saxophone, more items to buy, etc. Online shopping is dangerous, even for men. Everyone loves mail, but I admit to sending myself far too much.

I could hear a delivery man outside my apartment building waiting for me to go down and accept a parcel. There was no way he would wait for me to crawl down the stairs on my bum so I stuck my head out the window and hollered down.

"Hello! Is that package for me?" I called.

"Depends. Are you Yahya Al-Abed?" he shouted back up at me.

"That's me! Any way I can convince you to bring that up for me? I'm trapped up here with a broken leg." Not waiting for his response, I held out my key to the building and dropped it down to him. "Heads up!"

This box either had my new saxophone in it or was a "Get Well" package sent by a friend. The size was indicative of the latter. Either way, I really should stop dropping small pieces of metal from a third story window but it had become such a convenient habit. I could see the headlines now – "Disabled Man Assaults Unsuspecting Bystander."

Writing everything down in my notebook allowed me to sort out my professional goals as well. I spoke to my programme director who was able to extend my contract with my current employer. I could now recover without any added stress bogging me down. Still, that was only temporary employment and it was important for me to start looking for another position to ensure I wouldn't enter unemployment anytime soon after.

In fact, I had an interview scheduled for today for a new position at another hospital. Due to the state of my leg, I arranged to have a Skype interview, rather than visiting with them in person.

Suddenly I feel a rush of urgency as my notepad reminds me that my interview is in ten minutes and counting! I accept my new parcel and set it on the counter beside my prescription bottle – both unopened. I'd have to wait until this interview was over before I could open it.

I fall into my desk chair just as the call begins coming through on my computer.

During the formal greetings, I take the opportunity to thank my interviewer for speaking with me over Skype rather than in person and offered to explain why it was necessary since they were unaware of my condition. They were kind and considerate.

The initial questions were fairly standards and expected – Can you tell us about your training? Are you able to perform operations X, Y, and Z? Can you identify a mistake you've made in the past and how you've learned from it?

It wasn't until about 15 minutes in that the conversation shifted in a multifarious way as if someone had begun boiling the beaker. Adding a little bit of heat always makes things more interesting.

"Describe some challenges you've faced that you've felt have impeded your ability to do your job."

Oh, where do I begin? I'm tempted to address the critical shortage of coffee in the break rooms but opt to highlight a slightly more sophisticated issue instead.

"I'd have to say the unrealistic regulations forced on hospitals by government officials who wish to silence short-term cries from the public instead of looking for long-term solutions."

The interview raised his eyebrows and said nothing. The silence grew. That's not good. I've said too much already. "As you know, this interview is for a short-term contract." he said, after breaking the silence. "However, where do you see yourself in the long run?"

I pause a moment to think about my options. I've always thought that if I could not find the position I want, I might then leave the country alongside a slew of other professions in a modern day immigration move that'll strategically place me in an environment where I'm not forced to choose between providing optimal care and saving the government money. I wasn't the only one who saw our system slowly deteriorating.

I had already changed the tone of the interview with my answer to his last question but perhaps I could recover.

"My current plans are to stay here in London, but I wouldn't be opposed to entertaining the possibility of international positions. I'm always interested in opportunities that allow me to grow and improve."

"You don't find that to be the case here? Do you feel limited?" he probed.

"Sometimes." I replied. "I've learned a great deal during my time here, but I believe there's a win-win-win still yet to be found for everyone in the healthcare system, but instead of continuing to look for it, the government seems to want to withdraw its support (no doubt for reasons we can't fully comprehend) and quality is suffering because of it."

"Three wins? 'Win-win-win?'" the interviewer chuckles.

"Definitely!" I proclaim, more thrilled that he was wearing a smile now. "I count three separate groups of needs that should be met within the medical industry – the government, the country's citizens, and the medical professionals, like myself, who treat all of them. An argument could be made for a fourth group who develop products for the industry, but the main point that's becoming abundantly clear is that the healthcare system is lacking in the quality department, something I've personally been able to witness."

This interviewer wasn't giving me much feedback to work with. He nods and continues onward.

"We're looking for someone to start fairly soon. If we offer you the position, how quickly do you think you'd be able to join our team?

"That's a good question. At the moment, that's up to my own doctor to determine. I could be out for a few more weeks or a couple of months. I have another appointment scheduled in a week where I'll get an updated status report."

"Well, thank you for your time, Dr. Al-Abed. Hope you have a swift recovery and you'll hear back from us soon." The video call ended after a few more pleasantries were exchanged.

I leaned back in my chair, squinting at the blank computer screen while the ensuing silence was filled with the realisation that I had a small chance getting that position. I may have masked my caveman qualities by shaving for the first time in weeks, but other than that, I gave them every reason *not* to hire me. I was incapacitated and unsure of when I could resume work. Addressing my clear concerns about the

Catch-22 scenarios hospital management often force doctors into probably wouldn't help either. I wasn't ending that call with any high hopes for future employment.

I should have been more concerned about my performance but became preoccupied once again with my thoughts of the parcel still sitting unopened on my kitchen counter. It was from my friend over in Australia who knew I was picking up a few extra hobbies during my forced sabbatical form work and thought she'd send me a little project.

I picked up a folded card laying on top of some blue yarn.

"Prove you're a surgeon and knit me a rabbit. Angelica"

What?! I'm not *that* bored. I've certainly been creating on a long "To Do" list, but this is NOT one of the activities I had in mind. What was she trying to do, guarantee I go crazy?

10 Adapting

Several weeks down and only a few more to go. Having so much free time was unbearable in the beginning but now I was absolutely loving it. My time away from work was becoming a kind of forced meditation that was slowly changing my perspective on the value of these empty days. Learning to be patient with the healing process hasn't been easy for me. I accepted the fact that I wasn't fully functional as before but that didn't mean I had to stop having a sense of accomplishment.

The confidence I had performing my duties at work have shifted over to my personal life. I had a choice to make. And, rather than waste these precious moments by remaining lazy on the couch, I changed my perspective on time and took to my To Do list to a whole new level of enthusiasm. One by one, I had been attacking them with all the fervent dignity that I could muster. Including figuring out how to stay healthy by working out and eating healthy. That meant spending more time in the kitchen to satisfy my sweet tooth rather than ordering in.

My cravings had turned from bite-sized chocolate brownies to oven-baked goodies. I desperately wanted some muffins but I couldn't find the proper baking pans. My training at the hospital left few adventures to be had in the culinary world. I'm not exactly the cook I'd always wanted to be. I could blame work for most of my downfalls (easy target).

But, to be fair, I could also credit most of my successes to my career.

Leaving the combined ingredients mixing in a bowl, I continue my search for a muffin pan. It had been awhile since I had even opened some of these cupboards and half expected a surprise resident to jump out at me. Perhaps a baking pan was behind cupboard number one. Nope. In sequence, I open all the remaining cabinet doors. Still nothing. Leaning against the counter, I sip the last of my Diet Coke, allowing its contents to energize my creative juices.

"Eureka!" I grab a pair of scissors and begin cutting the can in half. "Voila!" I chuckle to myself. "I've got myself a muffin pan. Nothing can stop me!" I pour some batter into the bottom portion of the can and place it in the oven.

I embrace a sigh of victory as I look down at the medical boot now protecting my leg. Manoeuvring around the kitchen would have been substantially more difficult with my cast on. But enough time had passed that my doctor gave two thumbs up to have it removed. I was so excited that I didn't even feel bad for the guy who cut it off and received a full whiff of what seven weeks of not bathing your leg smells like. The casing around my leg reeked but I didn't care. He was probably used to it the way I'd grown accustomed to the smells of performing bowel surgeries.

118

Being a patient isn't easy but the continuity of care throughout physiotherapy with the same professionals made my transition much smoother. I hear that most people are forced to work with a new professional for every appointment they have, unable to figure out why these professionals keep giving them different advice or why they don't seem to fully understand their needs. I was lucky enough to have the same people working with me throughout my experience from the surgery by the orthopaedic surgeon to rehabilitation by the physiotherapist. No doubt, this was a huge key to me getting back into the swing of things quicker than expected.

The removal process slowly turned into a bittersweet moment as I realised my time away from work would soon be coming to a close. The cast turned out to be heavy in more ways than one. It was tasking learning how to carry this large mass around everywhere I went, bumping into doors, coffee tables and sometimes people. But, no sooner had it been removed then I began to feel the weight of the cast on my mind. Something I had originally viewed as a hindrance turned out to be a blessing in disguise, providing me the opportunity to see my daily settings from a new perspective I couldn't appreciate before.

No. I wouldn't want to go through it all again. There's nothing fun about falling ice and breaking bones. I genuinely enjoy surgeries but I'd rather be the one performing them rather than going under the scalpel. I used to think there was nothing worse than patients ignorantly complaining until I felt what it was like to be unsure of my own physical health. If I get a pick, I'll always choose the comfort of being in the loop rather than waiting for someone else to update me on *me*. I wouldn't ask for this accident to happen to me again, but I'm thankful for what I've found during this change of pace. When your immediate needs are met, it's easy to neglect or even ignore areas that need improvement in both your personal life and work life.

On that note, my leg wasn't completely free yet but a weight had definitely been lifted. I was given the confirmation I needed that everything was going to be alright and I could regain some of the physical control over my life before. Even though the bulkiness would have to stay because of the boot, I jumped at the opportunity to drive myself around the city before the cabin fever had another chance to settle in again. I had been unable to venture out of my apartment the way I normally would, friends occasionally taking me here or there. Finding a new restaurant or enjoying coffee with friends, these small pleasantries were a huge deal to be now. Even driving around with no purpose would be a considerable accomplishment so I grabbed at the chance to take my independence back.

A friend warned me that driving with a boot on may be illegal but neither my physiotherapist nor the local government websites could confirm or deny that. So, I did the only natural thing someone with a renewed sense of power would do. I took that lack of information as a sign of tacit compliance that I could now do whatever I pleased. If it was illegal, surely they would have said something or there'd be a pamphlet or two available. But, as luck would have it, it wasn't until I saw bright, flashing lights in my rear view mirror that I began regretting my decision.

I was caught just as I was arriving home from the grocery store, muffin ingredients in tow. I pulled into my parking spot and turned off the engine. I was already home! Why couldn't he just they me go? Frantic to hide the massive boot caging my leg, I quickly snatched my jacket from the passenger's seat and covered it up seconds before the police officer banged on my window.

"Are you crazy?!" he yells at me. "You did a dangerous manoeuvre!"

"What did I do wrong?" I asked calmly, unsure why screaming was necessary.

"Don't argue with me," he hisses back.

"I'm not arguing with you. You clearly saw something and I'm only asking what it was."

"You crossed through without looking!"

"That's not true." Oops. Bad choice of words. The policeman shoots a glare down at me.

I was right, though. Passing through the intersection, I most definitely had looked. If I should be in trouble for anything, my rolling stop would have been a better accusation. But, I wasn't about to change the subject with that kind of confession. There was no need to incriminate myself to such a large, burley police officer itching to punish me with any excuse.

My calm demeanour didn't seem to be any good at countering his aggression. This guy either hated the world in general or was already having the worst of days. Maybe he slipped on some ice and hurt himself. Who knows? But, no matter, I was scrambling for some alternate words.

"Look man," I continue. "I live here. I do this every single day. You can't pass this way without looking."

He stares down at me again, his expression showing no signs of sympathy or understanding. Without another word, he walks back to his car. I lean my head back against the headrest. This is just great. He's gone to discuss my impending doom with his partner. I was so close to my home but making a run for it was out of the question. If he asks me to get out of the car, he's going to see the boot on my leg and then there's no hope for me. This guy sounds like he's just one excuse away from arresting me.

I catch a glimpse of the policeman briskly making his way back over. How do I appeal to the humanity of a man who gives the impression that he hates most humans?

"Look. I'm sorry, man. I won't do it again."

"See that you don't," he mumbles. He gets back in his car and drives away.

I'm not sure what changed his mind, but there's no way I'm driving again until my leg is completely free. All it would take is one difficult cop and then who's going to hire a doctor who is interviewing from his jail cell? I doubt they'd find the humour in using a mug shot for my new hospital ID card.

From now on, if I needed fresh air, opening a window would have to be sufficient. One accident already got in the way of my future goals, I wasn't going to allow another one to happen. Staying home was the safer choice. Not an opinion I would normally adhere to, but it's only temporary. Plus, that gave me more time to hate being a patient, something I was beginning to love.

Beep! Beep! Beep! Just then, the oven timer snaps me out of my flashback. My muffins are done!

Just in time as my Italian friends Vincenzo and his wife came to visit me and see how I was recovering.

11 Back to Work

Over five months had passed since that wretched day on the ice. Although I had grown to have a whole new level of respect and patience for my own patients, I was thrilled (and much more comfortable) returning back to the professional end of the stethoscope.

My job interview had also gone much better than expected and I found myself walking down a set of hallways in my new hospital, on my way to see my first patient with my new employer. If my interviewer was comfortable with me voicing unhindered expressions of the country's current healthcare standards, values and the downward direction I thought things were going, these were people I didn't mind accepting a job from.

Reaching the recovery bay, I find my 35-year-old patient laying quietly in bed, surrounded by several of his family members and a cloud of mixed emotions. He had been admitted under the diagnosis that his fever and pain of two days were caused by an appendicitis. However, when he went under the knife, things turned out a little differently.

"Good morning! How's my patient handling their recovery?"

"Hello, Doctor," the man responds in a rather melancholy tone.

He didn't use my surname. He has no idea that I'm the one who performed surgery on him just a few hours prior. Not to mention, I'm probably the tenth hospital worker he's interacted with since his arrival and he's beginning to lose count of names and specialties. If his experience is anything like mine, he'll come into contact with at least a dozen more staff members before noon.

"What's taking so long?" the wife quickly chimes in. "We've been waiting for an eternity!"

This was a tad over-dramatic, but not without its merits. I may have changed hospitals but it's the same situation today as it was yesterday and the day before that. Patients are given the impression they'll receive immediate help in an emergency and they expect the punctuality of that service to continue throughout their stay. And when society's stereotypical image of medical perfection doesn't hold up, outrage ensues.

Part of their view has some validity. As professionals dealing with human lives, whose skill level often determines whether or not someone will walk out of a hospital, we should be held to a higher standard but that also means that we are unfairly caught in the crossfire of a battle between the government and its people; a rock and a hard place. Doctors have become so used to apologising for someone else's policies that even we can forget where the problem of diminished quality care originates.

"I'm sorry you've been waiting for so long," I say, shaking the wife's hand. "The flood of patients entering the hospital seems never ending but, if we work together well, I'm willing to let other people wait so I can properly meet your needs."

She nods only once, unsure of how to take my response.

Bypassing everyone else in the room, I approach the man's bed and lower my voice, not necessarily for privacy but to indicate my words were meant to focus on his needs above anyone else in the room. "I actually do understand how it feels having to wait for people to show up with some useful information. It's no fun but now that I've had the opportunity to collect all the relevant facts, I can give you a full briefing."

The man's mouth slowly begins to open in shock as I inform him that what first appeared to be a classic case of appendicitis actually turned out to be colon cancer.

"I have… cancer?" the man stutters.

"You *had* cancer," I was pleased to correct him. "As soon as we were provided a better look at what was causing your symptoms, we were able to clearly identify the areas of concern and it was completely removed."

"Completely?" he questions.

"Completely," I confirm. "You can count a healthy recovery."

His hesitation to believe me was understandable. There had only been a few minutes to digest life altering news. He walked into the hospital thinking one thing only to have one diagnosis turn into another.

The truth of the matter was even more complex than my patient could have imagined. He was lucky a specialist in colon surgery just happen to be working during his arrival. He was lucky to benefit from a free healthcare system. If the family's general appearance is any indication of their financial standing, they are lucky to live in a country where free healthcare is granted as a right. People in other parts of the world are often driven to bankruptcy, forced to empty out their savings for the future to address their medical needs of today. This is why this system is so beneficial and why it's important not to retreat backwards and withdraw this support but figure out a way to improve it.

Other countries like New Zealand, Australia, France, Canada, even Chile in South America have long been taking similar strides towards meeting the basic needs of their people. A shared remaining concern is the quality received. What could a country do to be distinctly set apart from the rest? Under what conditions could an economy allow that to happen?

I wish I had all the answers. I see how the people benefit and having been a patient, I've also experienced the downfalls still hindering the potential of a truly great system.

The influence the free healthcare system has on the economy is undeniable when people are healthy, functioning and don't have the fear that their basic needs won't be met. Not to mention that free at the point of use, universal healthcare is arguably a key characteristic of a fully developed and sophisticated nation.

Maybe the answer lies in developing a system where people feel they are funding their own healthcare savings rather than supporting everyone else around them. Perhaps the main focus of the equation has to do with decreasing demand rather than catering to current demand levels. I'll consider leaving the philosophical thought process to those with more data to work with. However, just because I don't have all the answers, this doesn't mean I'll stop thinking about all the positive contributions I can make. Hopefully, if others do the same, that will be enough to keep us moving in the right direction.

What will happen if things don't change and improvements aren't made? Would things get worse? I think back to the staking rink and wonder what would happen if the maintenance crew chose to save a few pounds and not smooth the ice over? The smallest of cracks are left to make astronomical consequences that will affect human lives.

The healthcare problems go much deeper than merely discussing bedside manner and the concept of eliminating the humanity from the practice of medicine. Instead this has become an issue of whether someone comes to your beside or not.

Patients want proof of subjective quality while the government wants proof of money saved. All the while, medical professionals are stuck in between desperately trying to come up with a differential diagnosis that will make both sides happy. The irritation of my patient's wife is a perfect example of how the public often feels about their healthcare system. Patients and their families just want to feel secure in always having their healthcare concerns addressed.

Just in case anyone begins to forget all the negative aspects of a free healthcare system, the media is on standby to remind them. It seems like a solid dose of propaganda, considering the government would substantially benefit from a financial perspective if it could stop spending billions on the NHS if the people began hating it enough. If they could get the public to beg for a private healthcare system, they'd be off the hook.

The interesting aspect of all this is that neither party is wrong. Everyone can agree that the golden goose of all healthcare systems is not working properly. What we don't agree on is why. All great plans can turn into a disaster if they aren't implemented correctly. Is there a middle ground where everyone (the government, the medical professionals and the public) can come together and have their priorities met? Is there a way to satisfy the needs of everyone? Do the leaders have the capabilities to prioritise their short-term goals with the public's long-term goals or is this simply something we need to ride out?

Yes. Perhaps. Questionable. And, no.

Nobody is certain which direction the healthcare system is going here, but many are counting on the quality getting much worse before it gets any better and professionals are adjusting their career paths accordingly, leaving the government and its people to do without.

These three groups, this tripod as a unit, determine the quality of care provided to the people, and if one breaks, the entire system fails. There's no stability with one of the legs leaving to practice in another country. Doctors are continuing to leave for environments they can feel supported in. The unfortunate reality of the matter is why would you stay when you could have something better? Why persevere when you could avoid the struggle altogether?

If my History Channel binge watching has cemented any major philosophy, it's that we can't go backwards and we won't benefit by standing still. Both choices would cause the public to miss out on something so beneficial to their well-being by jeopardising future accessibility. Next thing you know, the humanity side of medicine will be extinct and the power of human connection on a professional level will be forgotten.

What's true in the medical field holds true in the rest of life. Concentrating on the symptoms of a problem only provides temporary solutions to much deeper issues. Serious problems are enhanced by long wait times, outsourcing medical tasks, budget cutting and professionals leaving the country. Finding the root of the problem and rearranging our priorities is key to finding a workable solution to one of the nation's biggest problems.

In the meantime, it seems likely that the population will be subject to …

Medical Observational Assessment – Maintaining unattainable regulations and issuing budget cuts ensure high fines and social pressure. Decrease level of quality by increasing the percentage of temporary staff and outsourcing additional medical tasks. Likelihood of maintaining a high professional population – not likely. Treat unsatisfied patients with a dose of local media every 24 hours to solidify continued pain and scepticism of the quality of current care. Resuscitate as needed.

About the Author

Dr. Yahya Al-Abed, is a surgeon based in London. He had just completed specialist training in general and colorectal surgery, when a sudden sporting accident halted his career.

This book examines his struggle to accept a new role as a patient, deal with career uncertainties and grapple with loss of control.

In addition to his recent experience as a guest of the NHS, he has provided a unique perspective on the quality of the health industry, which is currently undergoing significant problems with funding, recruitment and morale.

Unmasked

Read additional, medical-related articles

by Dr. Yahya Al-Abed at:

www.PubMed.com

 GOLDEN ARROW PUBLISHING

Printed in Great Britain
by Amazon